Colin Kaepernick

By Jon M. Fishman

AMAZING ATHLETES

Lerner Publications Company • Minneapolis

Lerner Publications Company
A division of Lerner Publishing Group, Inc.
241 First Avenue North
Minneapolis, MN 55401 USA

For reading levels and more information, look up this title at www.lernerbooks.com.

Library of Congress Cataloging-in-Publication Data

Fishman, Jon M.
    Colin Kaepernick / by Jon M. Fishman.
      pages   cm. — (Amazing athletes)
    Includes index.
    ISBN 978–1–4677–3674–9 (lib. bdg. : alk. paper)
    ISBN 978–1–4677–4585–7 (eBook)
    1. Kaepernick, Colin—Juvenile literature. 2. Football players—United States—Biography—
Juvenile literature. I. Title.
GV939.K25F57 2015
796.332092—dc23 [B]   2014003641

Manufactured in the United States of America
1 – BP – 7/15/14

TABLE OF CONTENTS

Colin throws a pass in the first quarter of the game against the Green Bay Packers.

COLD STREAK

Quarterback Colin Kaepernick took the **snap** on January 5, 2014. His breath came out in thick, white clouds. It was only five degrees at Lambeau Field in Green Bay, Wisconsin. The wind made it feel even colder.

Colin and the San Francisco 49ers trailed the Green Bay Packers in the fourth quarter, 17–13. It was the first game of the **playoffs** for both teams. Green Bay is a tough team. The Packers had just won the Super Bowl in 2011. Green Bay's quarterback, Aaron Rodgers, is one of the biggest stars in the National Football League (NFL).

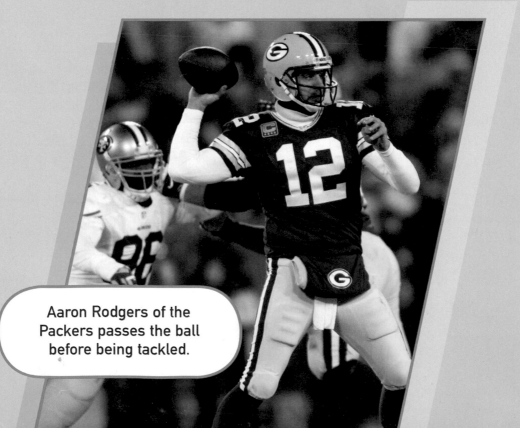

Aaron Rodgers of the Packers passes the ball before being tackled.

Colin looks for a teammate to catch his pass.

Many people thought the cold weather would be an advantage for the Packers. Green Bay is used to playing in snow and cold wind. But Colin didn't mind the icy air. He set a good example for his teammates. "I've played in cold-weather games before," Colin said. "I feel like it's more mental than anything."

Colin took two quick steps back. Then he hopped and launched the ball. It soared down the middle of the field. San Francisco **tight end** Vernon Davis was there. He caught the ball between two **defenders**. Touchdown! The 49ers took the lead, 20–17. But there was still plenty of time for Green Bay to catch up.

Some of the coldest games in NFL history have been played in Green Bay. It was 13 degrees below zero during the 1967 NFL championship between the Packers and the Dallas Cowboys!

The Packers drove down the field and kicked a **field goal**. The game was tied, 20–20. San Francisco took control of the ball again. There were five minutes and six seconds left in the game. Could the 49ers score?

Colin marched his team down the field. But San Francisco was still out of field goal range.

It was third down. Colin faked a deep pass. He scrambled to his left to avoid the Green Bay **blitz**. He streaked up the field for 11 yards. First down! The 49ers kicked a field goal a few plays later. They won the game!

San Francisco coach Jim Harbaugh was proud of his team. He was especially pleased with his star quarterback. "Colin Kaepernick, I think we can all agree, is a **clutch performer**," Coach Harbaugh said.

Jim Harbaugh *(right)* congratulates Colin *(left)* after a touchdown pass.

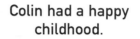

Colin had a happy childhood.

BUDDING STAR

Heidi Russo gave birth to a baby boy in Milwaukee, Wisconsin, on November 3, 1987. Russo was 19 years old at the time. She didn't feel ready to care for a baby. She gave her son up for **adoption**.

Colin *(center)* laughs with his parents before a game.

Colin Rand Kaepernick was six weeks old when he was adopted. Teresa and Rick Kaepernick already had a son named Kyle and a daughter named Devon. They added Colin to the family.

The Kaepernicks lived in Fond du Lac, Wisconsin. Colin fit right in with the family. But he doesn't look like his brother and sister. Russo, his birth mother, is white. Colin's birth father, whom he has never met, is African American. Colin has darker skin than the rest of his family.

"We've always been really open about the adoption, and we were always open about the skin colors," Teresa

Colin spent most of his childhood in Turlock, California.

said. "We pointed it out as a positive, and he saw his difference and was comfortable with it." In school, Colin was asked to draw a picture of his family. He used a brown crayon for himself and a yellow crayon for the rest of his family.

In 1991, Rick got a new job. The Kaepernicks moved to Turlock, California. Colin was four years old at the time.

The kids in this photo play football in a youth league, just like Colin did.

He already loved to play all kinds of sports. He was still too young for Little League baseball. But he followed his older brother to games and hung out in the **dugout**.

Colin joined a youth football team when he was eight. He became the team's quarterback in his second season. Colin's first pass in a game was a long touchdown. "Everyone in the stands sat there with their mouths open because at the time, nine-year-olds almost never passed," Teresa said. "He had an extremely strong arm."

Colin has had a pet **tortoise** named Sammy since he was 10 years old. The reptile weighs about 115 pounds!

Colin winds up for a pitch during a high school baseball game.

NFL DREAM

Colin's strong arm made him a force on football and baseball fields. He also enjoyed basketball. He played all three sports at John H. Pitman High School in Turlock.

Colin was growing fast. He stood six feet four inches tall by 2004. But the high school junior was also skinny. He weighed just 170 pounds. His slim frame affected the way his football coaches called plays for Colin. He usually threw the ball or handed it to **running backs**. He rarely ran with the ball himself. His coaches were afraid he'd get hurt.

Colin looks for a receiver during a 2006 football game.

The young quarterback showed promise on the football field. His best sport was probably baseball, though. He could pitch the ball as fast as 94 miles per hour. He threw two **no-hitters** as a senior in 2006. Colleges such as the University of Tennessee and Arizona State University offered Colin **scholarships**. They wanted him to pitch on their baseball teams.

But Colin had other hopes. Back when he was eleven years old, his teacher had asked him to write a letter. The letter was supposed to be about what he wanted to be doing with his life in seven years. Colin had written that he wanted to "go to

Colin loved to play baseball in high school. But he dreamed of playing professional football.

the pros and play on the Niners or the Packers even if they aren't good in seven years." Niners is a nickname for the San Francisco 49ers. Colin had

Turlock is in central California. It is about two hours east of San Francisco by car.

wanted to play in the NFL for a long time. He wasn't going to give up his dream so easily.

17

Kyle helped Colin seek a football scholarship. The brothers made phone calls. They sent DVDs highlighting Colin's skills to schools all around the country. Finally, the University of Nevada made an offer. Colin was going to play for the Nevada Wolf Pack.

There are many schools with more successful football programs than the University of Nevada. But Colin was happy to have found a team that valued his skills. "Looking back, it's almost satisfying it happened that way," Colin said later. "It was one team that trusted in me and wanted me."

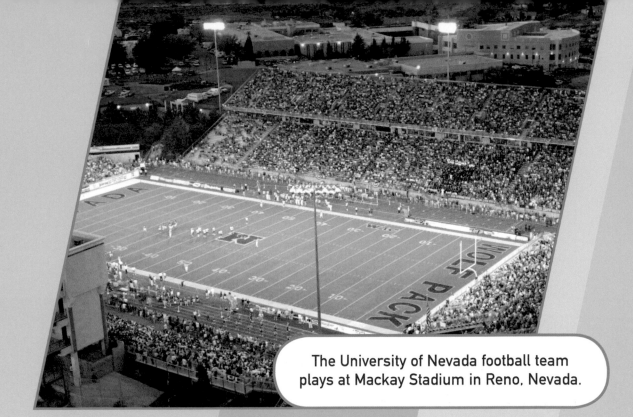

The University of Nevada football team plays at Mackay Stadium in Reno, Nevada.

ONE OF THE PACK

Colin wasn't quite ready to jump in as the starting quarterback at Nevada. He spent his first season on the bench as a **redshirt**. He practiced with his team and learned as much as he could. He also exercised and put on muscle.

When the 2007–2008 football season started, Colin was no longer the skinny kid who the coaches had to protect. He weighed 225 pounds and could take care of himself.

Nevada starting quarterback Nick Graziano was hurt. The team turned to Colin. He was named the starting quarterback against Boise State University on October 14, 2007. It was a wild game.

Colin *(right)* stretches for a touchdown while Boise State's Marty Tadman *(lower left)* looks on.

Both teams seemed to score at will. But Boise State came out on top, 69–67.

It was a disappointing loss for Nevada. The team was excited for their new quarterback, though. Colin had thrown for 243 yards

Colin runs for a first down in a game against Brigham Young University.

and three touchdowns in the game. Even more incredible, he had run for 177 yards and scored two more touchdowns.

Some baseball teams didn't want to give up on Colin. He was chosen by the Chicago Cubs in the 43rd round of the 2009 Major League Baseball (MLB) **draft**.

Most people hadn't expected Colin to be such a good runner. His high school coach, Brandon Harris, sure hadn't seen it coming. "You see him running like a banshee, so I finally asked him, 'Could you run like that [all along] and we just missed it?'" Coach Harris said. "I didn't know he'd be the runner he is now."

Colin was named the Wolf Pack's starting quarterback for the rest of the year. He finished the season with 19 touchdown passes. He threw just three **interceptions**. Colin was named Freshman of the Year in his **conference**.

Over the next three seasons, Colin proved that his freshman year was no fluke. He racked up stats and set record after record. He was named Western Athletic Conference (WAC) Offensive Player of the Year in 2008 and 2010. In four college seasons, he threw 82 touchdown passes. He also ran for an astonishing 59 touchdowns.

Colin outruns teammates and opponents alike during a 2008 game against Texas Tech.

Colin helps the Nevada Wolf Pack win a 2010 game as he runs for a touchdown.

SUPER BOWL SUPERSTAR

Colin had become known as a quarterback who runs a lot. Some people didn't think this style would work well in the NFL. They thought he would get hurt. NFL defenders are bigger, stronger, and faster than college players.

Partly because of his style, Colin wasn't chosen until the second round of the 2011 NFL Draft. The 49ers were excited about their new player. But the team already had a starting quarterback. Just like in college, Colin would have to wait for his chance. He didn't play much in 2011.

In 2012, Colin again began the season as the backup. But San Francisco's starting quarterback was hurt in a game against St. Louis in November.

Colin worked hard as the team's backup quarterback and was ready to play when needed.

Colin was named the starter for the next game against the Chicago Bears. He played well with two touchdown passes. The 49ers crushed the Bears, 32–7. Colin held on to the starting job for the rest of the season.

San Francisco kept on winning. They beat the Packers and the Atlanta Falcons in the playoffs. The 49ers were headed to the Super Bowl!

Colin has a lot of tattoos. He had some added to his chest three days after the Super Bowl. "They represent family, inner strength, humility, and spiritual growth," he said.

Colin threw for more than 300 yards in the big game. He also ran for a 15-yard touchdown. This is the longest touchdown run by a quarterback in Super Bowl history. But it wasn't enough. The Baltimore Ravens came out on top, 34–31.

It had been an amazing season for San Francisco. Colin had become a superstar around the world. People expected a lot out of the team in 2013–2014. After beating the Packers in the playoffs, Colin and the 49ers got past the Carolina Panthers, 23–10. They lost a week later, though, to a team with another quarterback known for running.

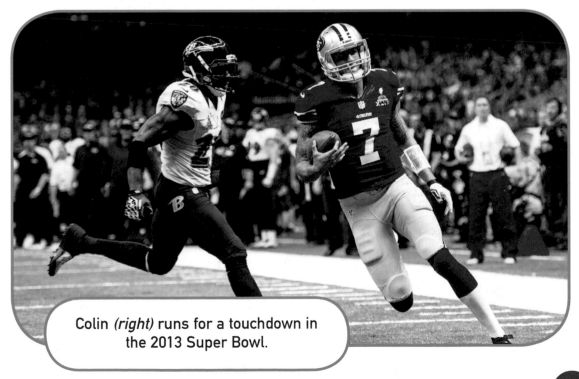

Colin *(right)* runs for a touchdown in the 2013 Super Bowl.

Russell Wilson and the Seattle Seahawks beat the 49ers to advance to the Super Bowl.

Colin has made the most of his time in the NFL. "When you have the opportunity . . . you have to take full advantage of it," he said. With his talent and drive, he'll likely get plenty more opportunities to shine on the field.

Even though Colin didn't play in the 2014 Super Bowl, he attended the *GQ* magazine Super Bowl party in style.

Selected Career Highlights

2013–2014 Finished fourth in the NFL in rushing yards by a quarterback (524)
Led the 49ers to the conference championship game

2012–2013 Finished fourth in the NFL in rushing yards by a quarterback (415)
Led the 49ers to the Super Bowl

2011–2012 Chosen by San Francisco with the 36th pick in the NFL draft

2010–2011 Named Offensive Player of the Year in his conference
Threw 21 touchdown passes and just 8 interceptions for Nevada

2009–2010 Threw 20 touchdown passes and just 6 interceptions for Nevada

2008–2009 Named Offensive Player of the Year in his conference
Threw 22 touchdown passes and just 7 interceptions for Nevada

2007–2008 Threw 19 touchdown passes and just 3 interceptions for Nevada

2006–2007 Played football, baseball, and basketball at John H. Pitman High School
Threw 25 touchdown passes and just 6 interceptions for Pitman

2005–2006 Played football, baseball, and basketball at John H. Pitman High School
Threw 13 touchdown passes and just 4 interceptions for Pitman

2004–2005 Played football, baseball, and basketball at John H. Pitman High School

2003–2004 Played football, baseball, and basketball at John H. Pitman High School

Glossary

adoption: to bring a child into a family to raise as one's own child

blitz: a rush of the quarterback by many defenders

clutch performer: an athlete who performs very well under pressure

conference: a group of college sports teams that play against one another

defenders: players who try to keep the other team from scoring

draft: a yearly event in which teams take turns choosing new players from a group

dugout: a shelter on the side of a baseball field where the players sit

field goal: a kick over the crossbar at either end of a football field during regular play. A field goal is worth three points.

interceptions: forward passes that are caught by the other team. The team that catches the interception takes control of the ball.

no-hitters: baseball games in which a pitcher pitches the whole game for his team and doesn't let the other team get a hit

playoffs: a series of games held to determine a champion

quarterback: a player whose main job is to throw passes

redshirt: a college athlete who is kept out of competition for a year. Redshirts can extend their time playing sports in college by one year.

running backs: players whose main job is to run with the ball

scholarships: money awarded to students to help pay college tuition

snap: to start a football play by handing or tossing the ball to a quarterback or running back

tight end: a player at the end of the offensive line who blocks and catches passes

tortoise: a type of very large turtle that lives on land

Further Reading & Websites

Fishman, Jon M. *Russell Wilson*. Minneapolis: Lerner Publications, 2015.

Kennedy, Mike, and Mark Stewart. *Touchdown: The Power and Precision of Football's Perfect Play*. Minneapolis: Millbrook Press, 2010.

Official NFL Site
http://www.nfl.com
The NFL's official website provides fans with recent news stories, statistics, biographies of players and coaches, and information about games.

Official San Francisco 49ers Site
http://www. 49ers.com
The official website of the 49ers includes team schedules, news, profiles of past and present players and coaches, and much more.

Savage, Jeff. *Aaron Rodgers*. Minneapolis: Lerner Publications, 2012.

Sports Illustrated Kids
http://www.sikids.com
The *Sports Illustrated Kids* website covers all sports, including football.

Index

Photo Acknowledgments

The images in this book are used with the permission of: © Ronald Martinez/Getty Images, p. 4; © Michael Zagaris/San Francisco 49ers/Getty Images, pp. 5, 6, 8; Seth Poppel Yearbook Library, pp. 9, 16; AP Photo /Patrick Cummings, p. 10; © Modesto Bee/ZUMApress.com/Alamy, p. 11; © iStockphoto.com/ActionPics, p. 12; © Tony Brunsman, pp. 14, 17; Icon SMI /Newscom, p. 19; AP Photo/Matt Cilley, p. 20; AP Photo/George Frey, p. 21; AP Photo/Tim Dunn, p. 23; © Ethan Miller/Getty Images, p. 24; © Ezra Shaw /Getty Images, pp. 25, 29; © Tringali/SportsChrome/Getty Images, p. 26; © Craig Barritt/Getty Images, p. 28.

Front cover: © Otto Greule Jr./Getty Images.

Main body text set in Caecilia LT Std 55 Roman 16/28.
Typeface provided by Adobe Systems.

Colin K...

When San Francisco 49ers quarterback Colin Kaepernick was in high school, his coaches thought he was too skinny to play in college. At the University of Nevada, his coaches thought he ran with the ball too often and he would be prone to injury in the National Football League (NFL). But Colin led the 49ers to the 2013 Super Bowl. In 2014, he and his teammates were just one win away from playing in the big game again. Learn more about one of the biggest stars in the NFL.

$7.95 USA

ISBN 978-1-4677-4491-1

50795

9 781467 744911

sroom™
Group